ONLY SUCCESSFUL WAY OF HAILING A STREET CAR.

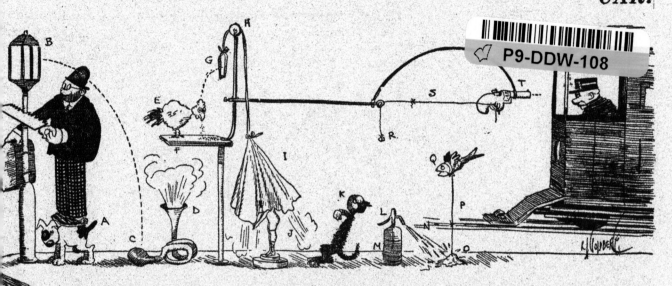

STAND ON RUSSIAN CAVIAR-HOUND (A) AND SAW LAMPPOST IN HALF - TOP (B) FALLS ON RUBBER BULB (C) BLOWING AUTOMOBILE HORN (D) AND FRIGHTENING CHICKEN (E) WHICH IS PEACEFULLY EATING LUNCH ON PLATFORM (F) - CHICKEN JUMPS, CATCHING HER NECK IN NOOSE (G) AND CHOKING INTO UNCONSCIOUSNESS - THE WEIGHT OF HER BODY PULLS ROPE OVER PULLEY (H) LIFTING CLOTH (I) AND UNVEILING STATUE OF EUROPEAN BATHING GIRL (J) - CAT (K) IS SHOCKED AT SIGHT AND FALLS BACK ON NECK (L) OF SODA SYPHON (M) STARTING FLOW OF SODA WATER (N) - SODA WATER SOFTENS GLUE (O) WHICH HOLDS FLYING FISH (Q) IN CAPTIVITY BY STRING (P) - AS GLUE SOFTENS, FISH IS RELEASED AND FLIES AT BREAD CRUMB (R) PULLING STRING (S) AND FIRING OFF PISTOL (T) WHICH PUTS MOTORMAN OUT OF BUSINESS - BY THE TIME THE COMPANY CAN GET ANOTHER MOTORMAN YOU ARE SAFELY ON THE CAR.

The Only Sanitary Way to Lick a Postage Stamp

TWO WEEKS BEFORE YOU WISH TO MAIL LETTER BUY A TURTLE AND PLACE HIM ON PLATFORM (A) WHICH IS SPRINKLED WITH TURTLE FOOD - WHEN TURTLE TRAVELS TO POSITION (B) IN TWO WEEKS' TIME, PULL STRING (C) WHICH THROWS ONION (D), AS IN DIAGRAM, HITTING TURTLE ON HEAD - THE BLOW TOGETHER WITH NATURAL STRENGTH OF ONION, MAKES TURTLE CRY - TEARS FALL ON POSTAGE STAMP, MAKING IT READY FOR USE.

For everyone who draws outside the lines
—S. A.

For Isidore and Jo
—R. N.

BEACH LANE BOOKS
An imprint of Simon & Schuster Children's Publishing Division · 1230 Avenue of the Americas, New York, New York 10020 · Text copyright © 2019 by Sarah Aronson · Illustrations copyright © 2019 by Robert Neubecker · All rights reserved, including the right of reproduction in whole or in part in any form. · BEACH LANE BOOKS is a trademark of Simon & Schuster, Inc. · For information about special discounts for bulk purchases, please contact Simon & Schuster Special Sales at 1-866-506-1949 or business@simonandschuster.com. · The Simon & Schuster Speakers Bureau can bring authors to your live event. For more information or to book an event, contact the Simon & Schuster Speakers Bureau at 1-866-248-3049 or visit our website at www.simonspeakers.com.
Book design by Lauren Rille
The text for this book was set in Quattro Tempi.
The illustrations for this book were rendered in number-two pencil and ink and then on a Macintosh computer.
Manufactured in China · 1218 SCP
First Edition
10 9 8 7 6 5 4 3 2 1
Library of Congress Cataloging-in-Publication Data · Names: Aronson, Sarah, author. | Neubecker, Robert, illustrator. · Title: Just like Rube Goldberg : the incredible true story of the man behind the machines / Sarah Aronson ; illustrated by Robert Neubecker. · Description: First edition. | New York : Beach Lane Books, 2019. | Includes bibliographical references. | Audience: Ages 3-8. | Audience: K to Grade 3. · Identifiers: LCCN 2018016834 | ISBN 9781481476683 (hardcover : alk. paper) | ISBN 9781481476690 (e-book) · Subjects: LCSH: Goldberg, Rube, 1883-1970–Juvenile literature. | Cartoonists–United States–Biography–Juvenile literature. · Classification: LCC NC1429.G46 A88 2019 | DDC 741.5/6973 [B] –dc23 LC record available at https://lccn.loc.gov/2018016834

Written by
Sarah Aronson

Illustrated by
Robert Neubecker

Just Like RUBE GOLDBERG

The Incredible True Story
of the Man Behind the Machines

Beach Lane Books · New York London Toronto Sydney New Delhi

Question: How do you become a successful, award-winning artist and famous inventor without ever inventing anything at all? (This is not a trick question.)

A man named **Rube Goldberg** did it! In a funny way, his life was just like one of his famous inventions: an improbable and inefficient chain reaction that ends up making perfect sense.

From the time he was a boy, Rube Goldberg loved to draw.
We're not just talking about simple stuff here.
As early as four years old, Rube traced the cartoons
he found in his books.
At eleven, he took official art classes from a sign painter.

Rube might have been a quiet boy.
He might have been shy.
But he was determined to be a great cartoonist
for a big-time newspaper.

Unfortunately, when he told his family, they were absolutely horrified! Beyond dismayed! Rube's father, Max, had emigrated from Germany to America to give his family a chance for a better life. He didn't want his son to end up a beggar on the streets.

He didn't enjoy mapping sewer pipes either. And he wasn't very impressed with the city's government. Rube still wanted to draw comics for a big-time newspaper.

Rube detested shoveling tunnels in mines two thousand feet underground.

So after six months he quit engineering and started over.

He got a job at the *San Francisco Chronicle*.

For eight dollars a week,
Rube emptied wastebaskets,
cleaned the floors, and
filed photographs in the
document morgue.

And whenever he had a chance,
Rube drew.

And drew.

And drew.

Day after day, Rube submitted his cartoons to the editor. Night after night, the editor mostly said no. When he said yes, Rube sometimes got paid, but other times he just got out of the office tasks he didn't like to do.

After a year, Rube convinced the sports department of the *San Francisco Bulletin* to hire him, and after that, he was a little more successful. He developed his style. The paper ran his cartoons. A column, too!

This might have been the (next) end of the story, but then the ground shook—literally.

The 1906 earthquake in San Francisco crumbled the city
and left many people without jobs and homes.
In the wake of disaster, it can be hard
for people to focus on their dreams.

It can be even harder to feel hopeful.

But Rube didn't give up on his dream.
Instead, he did the only thing he could do:
He drew comics to cheer people up.

And then he made a big decision.

In 1906, there was only one place where a guy like Rube could really make it big. It was the place he called the "front row," the cartoon capital of the country: New York City. So he got on a train and headed east.

He didn't have much—two hundred dollars and a diamond ring. (The ring was a gift from his father, just in case Rube needed to sell it to buy a ticket back home.)

After twelve days of pounding the pavement, lugging his
art from newspaper to newspaper, Rube did it! He got a job
as a cartoonist at a big-time paper: the *New York Evening Mail.*

Right off the bat, Rube became a celebrity.
Readers couldn't wait to see what he had to say
about all kinds of things.

Like sports.

And politics.

And the silliness of everyday life.

But maybe more than anything else, everyone loved reading about Rube's alter ego, Professor Lucifer Gorgonzola Butts.

The eccentric professor invented one intricate machine after another, and none of them were straightforward. In fact, they were the opposite of straightforward and often disregarded the laws of physics.

Although this was the age when new machines were being invented to make life easier, Rube's screwball contraptions purposefully solved problems in the most surreal and ridiculous ways.

Just like the machines
he studied in engineering school,
these complicated contraptions required lots
and lots of parts. And they always worked—on paper, of course.

They weren't practical in the real world—but that was never the point.
Rube Goldberg didn't draw machines that solved real-world problems.
He drew comics to make us look closer. And question logic. And tickle
the imagination.

And because of that, these machines accomplished something astounding
and more important than any pile of nuts and bolts ever could.

They challenged people to use the most amazing machine in the universe:

the brain!

So let's take it from the top: Rube
Goldberg became a stubborn, smart,
serious-about-being-funny engineer,
office boy, cartoonist, commentator,
comic genius, and award-winning
artist and inventor whose name is now
an adjective in the actual dictionary
without inventing a thing.

Is this kind of thing still possible?

You bet it is.

Figure out what you want. Work as
hard as you can. And most of all,
have a great time getting there. . . .

Just like Rube Goldberg!

Got more questions about Rube Goldberg?

Rube Goldberg was born on the fourth of July in 1883. His full name was Reuben Garrett Lucius Goldberg. He was a shy, serious boy with enormous ears. His parents were middle-class Jewish immigrants. His father, who originally thought that artists were not much more than beggars, eventually became his agent. When Rube studied at Berkeley, he drew cartoons for the *Pelican*, the student paper.

From 1905 to 1938, Rube created more than sixty original cartoon series, including *Foolish Questions*, *Mike and Ike*, and *Bobo Baxter*. For *I'm the Guy*, he encouraged readers to send in suggestions that led to gags like "I'm the guy who put the sand in sandwich." His first invention cartoon was "The Simple Mosquito Exterminator—No Home Should Be Without It." It appeared on July 17, 1912. It was anything but simple. From 1912 to 1932, Rube created a new invention nearly every two weeks, and then somewhat less often until 1964. Each composition could take as many as thirty hours to finish. Rube said his contraptions were "a symbol of man's capacity for exerting maximum effort to accomplish minimal results." The children's game Mouse Trap was inspired by his inventions. (And it actually worked!)

Rube loved cars. He acquired his first car, a Minerva, in 1910. He was one of the first people in New York City to own one.

Rube did not shy away from politics and controversy. He traveled to Paris four days after the outbreak of World War I to observe what the *Evening Mail* called "history at close range." He went to Europe in 1918 to cover the peace conferences. In 1939 he drew a contraption that made fun of Franklin Delano Roosevelt's New Deal. During World War II he received angry mail and death threats, so he asked his sons to change their last name. Tom chose the last name of George, which was a bit unfortunate, since his brother's first name was George.

Rube was known as the "dean of cartoonists." In 1946, after touring the country with other cartoonists to entertain the troops, Rube helped found the National Cartoonists Society and was elected its first president. In 1967 the society awarded him its highest honor—his namesake, the Reuben. In 1980 he was posthumously awarded the National Cartoonists Society Gold Key. In 1995 the US Postal Service made a stamp honoring "Rube Goldberg Inventions" that depicted his self-operating napkin.

In 1948 Rube received the Pulitzer Prize for his political cartoon "Peace Today," which shows a house and family perched on top of a gigantic atomic bomb, teetering between world control and world destruction.

Rube didn't believe in retirement. During his life he drew approximately 50,000 cartoons. At the age of eighty he even became a sculptor. Rube Goldberg died on December 7, 1970. He was eighty-seven.

Rube Goldberg wrote, "You have to have courage to be a creator." His work continues to inspire classrooms, cartoonists, and artists around the world to think outside the lines.

Sources

"11 Brilliant Rube Goldberg Machines." *Cool Material*. Dartboard Media LLC. Accessed April 3, 2017. coolmaterial.com/roundup/rube-goldberg-machines/.

"About Rube Goldberg." *Rube Goldberg, Unofficial Website*. www.rube-goldberg.com.

Beschloss, Steven. "Object of Interest: Rube Goldberg Machines." *New Yorker*. July 19, 2013. https://www.newyorker.com/tech/elements/object-of-interest-rube-goldberg-machines.

"The Genius of Rube Goldberg with Jennifer George, Al Jafee, and Adam Gopnik." Filmed March 10, 2014, at 92nd Street Y, New York, NY. Livestream video, 56:15. https://livestream.com/92Y/RubeGoldberg.

George, Jennifer, editor. *The Art of Rube Goldberg: (A) Inventive (B) Cartoon (C) Genius*. New York: Abrams ComicArts, 2013.

Ivey, Jim. "The Many Comic Adventures of Rube Goldberg." *Nemo: The Classic Comics Library*. February 1987.

Marzio, Peter C. *Rube Goldberg: His Life and Work*. New York: Harper & Row, 1973.

Popova, Maria. "The Art of Rube Goldberg." *Brain Pickings*. November 2, 2015, https://www.brainpickings.org/2013/12/04/the-art-of-rube-goldberg/.

Rube Goldberg Inc. "History of Rube Goldberg." The Amazing Rube Goldberg. Created September 1999. www.mousetrapcontraptions.com/history-4.html.

Rube Goldberg Inc. Rube Goldberg Machine Contest. https://www.rubegoldberg.com.

Tumey, Paul C. "Rube Goldberg." *The Masters of Screwball Comics* (blog). 2016. screwballcomics.blogspot.com/p/rube-goldberg.html.

Wolfe, Maynard Frank. *Rube Goldberg: Inventions*. New York: Simon & Schuster, 2000.

EASY WAY TO KEEP THE MILK FROM BEING STOLEN OFF THE FRONT STEP.

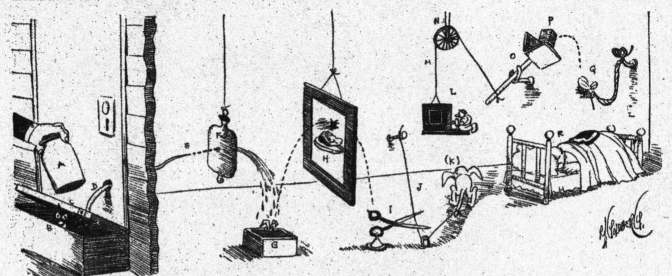

As thief lifts milk bottle (A) from door-step, cat (B) raises back, lifting door step(C) which pushes pointed rod(D) through door - point (E) punctures hot-water bag (F) causing water to fall on onion growing in box (G) - water causes onion to grow until it is strong enough to move around - onion spies picture of steak (H) and thinking it is the real thing, jumps up to embrace it - onion goes through canvass and falls on scissors (I) causing it to cut string (J) releasing watch dog (K) - watch dog attacks image of safe cracker (L) moving string (M) over pulley (N) and lifting hod (O). Brick (P) falls on captive bee (Q) - bee, thinking man (R) threw the brick, stings him and wakes him up in time to call up the police department and have the thief arrested.

ONLY KNOWN METHOD OF ATTRACTING A WAITER'S ATTENTION.

Before entering restaurant get an alcohol shampoo - fumes (A) from alcohol on head, rise and get horse-fly (B) soused - horse-fly staggers down trough (C) and falls on button (D) lighting cigar-lighter (E) setting off fire-crackers (F) - French pancake (G) hears noise of fireworks and thinks it a flock of zeppelins overhead. Jumps off platform with suicidal intent rather than be destroyed by enemy, pulling string (H) and sliding cover (I) from can (J) - insane doll (K) falls out - squirrel (L) sees nut and tries to get out of revolving cage (M), turning pulley (N) and setting glass cylinder (O) in motion - coins (P) inside of cylinder start jingling and sweet sounds of ready money reach waiter's ear through horn (Q) thus leading him to seek the source whence come the glad tidings.